CHARLIE BROWN'S 'CYCLOPEDIA

Super Questions and Answers and Amazing Facts

Featuring
All Kinds of Animals
from Fish to Frogs

Volume 2

Based on the Charles M. Schulz Characters

Funk & Wagnalls, Inc.

Photograph and Illustration Credits: Jane Burton/Bruce Coleman, Inc., ix; Copyright © 1972 by Follett Publishing Company, 54, 58, 61, 63, 83, 92, 93, reprinted from *Science for Human Value.*

3 4 5 6 7 8 9 0

A large part of the material in this volume was previously published in *Charlie Brown's Super Book of Questions and Answers.*

Introduction

Welcome to volume 2 of *Charlie Brown's 'Cyclopedia!* Have you ever wondered how fireflies light up, or how the shark got its name, or whether you can eat sea cucumbers? Charlie Brown and the rest of the *Peanuts* gang are here to help you find the answers to these questions and many more about all kinds of animals from fish to frogs. Have fun!

About the Animal Kingdom

How many different kinds of animals are there?

No! There are a lot more than that. More than one million kinds of animals live on the earth. When we think of animals, we usually think of our pets, the animals on a farm, and the animals in a zoo. We forget the creatures that live in the ocean. We forget insects, worms, and spiders. We even forget birds. They are all animals, too.

To a scientist, an animal is anything that is alive but is not a plant. The list of animals includes creatures that are so tiny we can see them only under a microscope. And the list includes you, too!

How smart are animals?

No other animals are as smart as people. But some are very intelligent. Apes, monkeys, and dolphins are the smartest. They can learn to do many things. Some of them can even solve problems. For example, a dolphin in a tank was once playing catch with a feather. One time the feather stuck to the side of the tank, high above the water. The game seemed to be over. But the dolphin figured out how to get the feather back. It jumped up and brushed the feather loose with the side of its head. The dolphin had solved its problem, and the game could go on. Most animals are not nearly this smart. Animals such as clams, crabs, insects, and worms are the least intelligent of all. They can't learn to do very much. Some can't learn anything.

What are instincts?

Animals are born knowing how to do certain things. A bird is born knowing how to build a nest. A fish is born knowing how to swim. A spider is born knowing how to spin a web. No one has to teach the animals to do these things. We say that the animals have an instinct for doing them. Instincts are not a sign of intelligence. When an animal acts from instinct, it does not have to learn anything or solve a problem.

Do animals talk to each other?

Yes, animals do talk to each other, but with "animal talk," not human talk. Animals do not use words and sentences the way people do. They express ideas and feelings to each other by using movements, smells, and sounds. A honeybee does a kind of dance to tell other honeybees where to find nectar. A female wolf gives off a certain smell that tells a male wolf she is ready to mate. A kitten meows to its mother to let her know it is hungry. A bird sings to warn other birds to keep away from its nest. These are all ways that animals talk to each other. Another animal of the same kind will understand the feeling or idea being expressed.

Some scientists think that dolphins may be able to talk the way humans do. But so far no one has proved that they can.

You can sometimes hear a lion's roar ten miles away!

How long do animals live?

The longest-living animal is probably the tortoise. We think it may live more than 150 years. At the other extreme is the mayfly, which lives only a few hours. The other animals are in between. An elephant can live 60 or 70 years. Your dog or cat will live about 12 or 15 years. A rat or mouse will live only 2 or 3 years. Some people say there are parrots that have lived more than 100 years, but no one has proved they do. Parrots can probably live about 50 years. So can geese, swans, and alligators. Rattlesnakes can live up to 18 years, but garter snakes don't usually live more than 5 or 6 years. People live about as long as elephants—around 70 years.

I DON'T SEE ANY GRAY HAIRS !

51

What is the biggest animal?

The biggest animal in the world is the blue whale. Some blue whales have grown as long as 109 feet and have weighed 150 tons!

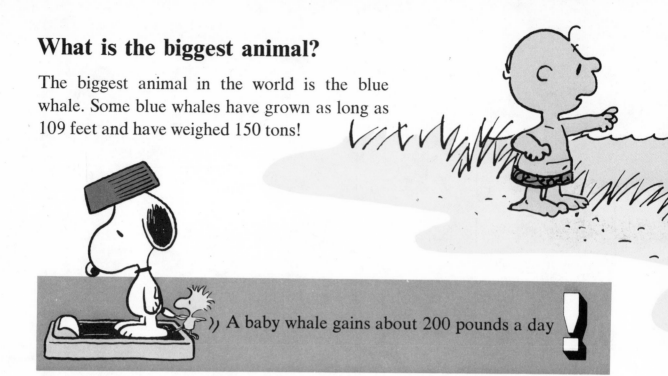

A baby whale gains about 200 pounds a day !

Why do some animals sleep all winter?

Many animals—such as the woodchuck—sleep all winter because they can't find food then. The plants that they eat die or lose their leaves when the weather gets cold. These animals eat a lot before winter comes, and grow fat. Then they sleep—or hibernate—inside a deep hole. They live all winter on the fat stored in their bodies. When spring comes, warmth and hunger wake up the sleepers.

Other animals, such as snakes, hibernate to escape cold weather. When the temperature is low, these animals slow down and can hardly move at all. If they stayed outside, they would freeze. So they spend the winter sleeping in a protected place.

52

What animals sleep all winter?

The winter sleepers include the ground squirrels, woodchucks, some bats, and jumping mice. Other animals, such as the bear, skunk, chipmunk, and badger, sleep part of the winter. They come out on days when the air isn't very cold. Many toads, turtles, snakes, frogs, and salamanders and some insects also hibernate.

What is the fastest animal?

The fastest of all animals is a bird called the swift. The spine-tailed swift can fly at a speed of more than 100 miles an hour. The word "swift" means fast, so there's no question about how this bird got its name.

The fastest land animal is the cheetah. It can run at more than 60 miles an hour.

53

How do animals live in the desert?

A desert is a very dry place. Animals that live there cannot always find water. But many small desert animals don't have to drink any water. They get all they need by eating desert plants. These plants have water stored in them.

During the day, most desert animals stay underground or in the shade. The hot sun would make them sweat. They would lose much of the water in their bodies. Instead, these animals come out at night, when the desert is cool. Then they don't sweat.

The camel gets along in another way. The camel must drink water. But once it has drunk, it can go for days without drinking any more. Its body is made especially for storing a lot of water. The camel can stay out in the hot sun because it sweats very little. So it does not lose the water stored in its body.

How do mother animals know their own babies?

By their smell. When a baby animal is born, its mother sniffs it and remembers the smell. From then on, whenever the mother wants to find her baby, she will sniff all the babies around until she finds the right one.

What are tails for?

The tails of animals are good for many things. A cow uses its tail as a fly swatter when it swishes away pesty insects. A fox wraps itself up in its tail to keep warm. A beaver slaps its flat tail on the water to give a warning signal. A fish uses its tail to help it swim. A squirrel uses its tail as a parachute when it jumps through treetops. A spider monkey can wrap its tail around a branch, and swing.

 A lizard called the gecko can drop its tail and grow a new one!

Why are there zoos?

Zoos were started so that people could see animals from strange, faraway places. Many people would never see zebras, elephants, peacocks, emus, and gnus if there were no zoos. Today we have zoos for other reasons, too. We keep them as places to raise and protect animals that are dying out.

Why do some animals die out?

In the past 200 years people have caused many kinds of animals to die out—to become extinct. People keep building houses and factories in fields and woods. As they spread over the land, they destroy animals' homes. If the animals can't find a place to live, they die out. Sixteen kinds of Hawaiian birds have become extinct for this reason. Other animals, such as the Florida Key deer, may soon die out because they are losing their homes. Hunters have caused some animals to become extinct, too. In the last century, hunters killed all the passenger pigeons in North America and most of the buffaloes. Today they are fast killing off hawks and wolves.

Pollution is killing many animals today, too. As rivers become polluted, fish are poisoned. Many die. Birds that eat the poisoned fish can't lay strong, healthy eggs. New birds aren't born. So far, no kinds of animals have become extinct because of pollution. But some, such as the bald eagle and the brown pelican, have become rare and may die out.

Scientists think that some animals become extinct because of changes in climate. The places where they live become hotter or cooler, drier or wetter. The food that they usually eat cannot grow there any more. If the animals can't learn to eat something else, they die. Dinosaurs may have died out for this reason.

Animals with No Bones

Are there animals that don't have any bones?

Yes. Insects, worms, and many animals that live in the sea have no bones. Most of these animals do have some hard parts. But these parts are on the outside of their bodies. The hard parts protect the animals' soft insides.

What are sea shells?

Sea shells are the hard, protective cases that certain sea animals form around themselves. Oysters, mussels, clams, scallops, and snails are all animals that have shells.

The sea shells you find sometimes have living animals inside. But usually the shells are empty by the time you get to them. The animals have been eaten by other sea animals or by sea gulls. The shells are often pretty, and it's fun to take them home.

Can you hear the sea in a sea shell?

No, you can't. When you hold a large spiral-shaped shell to your ear, you hear a roar. But it's not the roar of the sea. The shape of the shell makes any slight sound in the air echo back and forth inside the shell. Sounds that you may not normally hear are picked up by the shell and made louder.

The shell of a giant clam may weigh up to 600 pounds!

How does an oyster make a pearl?

Sometimes a little grain of sand gets inside the shell of a pearl oyster. The sand rubs against the soft body of the oyster. To stop the rubbing, the oyster wraps the sand in layer after layer of the same shiny coating it makes to line its shell. We call this coating mother-of-pearl. Gradually the bit of sand is wrapped in so many layers that a little ball forms. This ball is a pearl.

What happens if you grab a crab by one leg?

If the crab doesn't pinch you, it will probably let its leg drop off! The crab will run away, and you will be left holding the leg in your hand. Dropping a leg is the crab's way of protecting itself from you or any other danger. The crab can easily grow a new leg to replace the one it left behind.

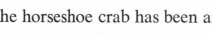 The horseshoe crab has been around for 500 million years!

What is a sponge?

A sponge is a sea animal with a soft, elastic skeleton. The animal has no legs, arms, fins, or stomach, and it doesn't move around at all. For many years people thought the sponge was really a plant. The soft skeleton of a dead sponge can hold a lot of water, so people have long used sponges for cleaning. But today, the sponge you use to wipe your kitchen counter is probably made in a factory.

Why does an octopus squirt black ink into the water?

An octopus squirts black ink into the water in order to hide from an enemy. That enemy may be a shark, a whale, or a person.

What does an octopus do with its eight arms?

An octopus uses its eight arms to catch crabs, clams, lobsters, and other shellfish. It also uses its arms to break open their shells, so it can eat them. On the underside of each arm are round muscles that act like suction cups. They can hold onto anything the octopus catches.

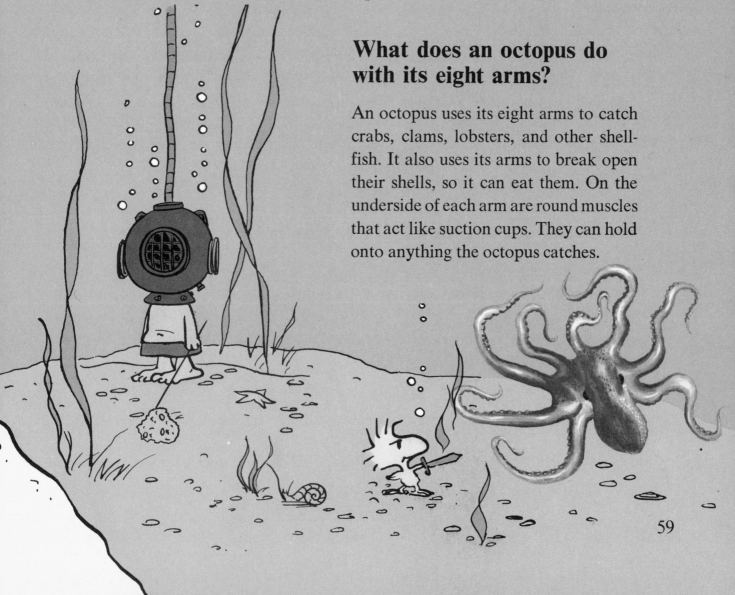

The basket starfish has more than 80,000 arms!

Why do jellyfish sting?

Jellyfish sting in order to get food. A jellyfish is a sea animal with a soft body and no shell. It eats other sea animals. First it paralyzes a small animal with its sting. Because the animal cannot move, the jellyfish can grab it and eat it. When you are swimming in the ocean, you may bump into a jellyfish and get stung. The sting may hurt, but you won't be paralyzed. So don't worry—the jellyfish will never eat *you*!

What sea animal looks like a flower?

The sea anemone (uh-NEM-uh-nee) looks like a flower, or at least like some sort of plant. It is a simple animal—just a hollow tube with a mouth at one end and a lot of wavy "arms" around the mouth. The arms are used to capture food. Sea anemones come in a variety of colors—red, green, brown, and orange. Some have dots and some have stripes.

IT'S CALLED A SEA ANEMONE!

60

Can you eat a sea cucumber?

Yes, but it doesn't taste like the cucumber you eat in a salad. A sea cucumber is not a vegetable. It is an animal that lives in the sand at the bottom of the sea. It was named "sea cucumber" because it is long and thin and looks much like a cucumber. However, it changes its shape all the time as it moves around. Sometimes it is very long and very skinny. Sometimes it is short and fat. Sometimes it is fat at both ends and skinny in the middle. Sea cucumbers are used in Oriental cooking. You can find them on the menu in some Chinese restaurants.

How do snails walk?

Snails have no legs, but they do have a foot. The whole bottom part of a snail's body is one smooth, flat foot. It moves the snail along the ground. As the snail moves, its foot gives off a slimy liquid. The liquid helps the snail to move more easily.

If you cut a starfish in pieces, each piece will grow into a whole starfish!

What happens to an earthworm when it is cut in two?

You might expect that the worm would die, but it doesn't always. A worm's body is one long row of sections that are all pretty much the same. A worm can lose a few of these sections without dying.

When a worm is cut into two pieces, the pieces wiggle around for a while. But they do not become two separate worms. The smaller piece usually dies. The larger piece can usually grow back the sections it lost—if it lost just a few.

VERY INTERESTING!

How long was the longest earthworm ever found?

The longest earthworm was even longer than two feet. It was nine feet long!

Insects

How many insects are there in the world?

A lot! Scientists say that there are about as many insects in one square mile of fertile land as there are people on the whole earth. So just think how many insects there might be in 100 square miles, in 1,000 square miles, and in the entire world!

What is an insect?

An insect is a very small animal with six legs. Many insects have two feelers and four wings, but others don't. There are many, many thousands of kinds of insects. They all look a little different. Such animals as flies, ants, bees, cockroaches, beetles, crickets, and butterflies are insects.

Where do all the insects come from?

They come from eggs. Female insects lay hundreds or even thousands of eggs during their lives. For example, a queen bee does nothing all summer but lay eggs. On any one day she may lay as many as 1,500. A female termite lays even more. She can lay as many as 30,000 eggs in one day!

If every insect hatched and lived its full life, the world would be overrun with insects. There would be no room for anyone else. Fortunately for us, many animals eat insects and insect eggs. Most insects never have a chance to grow up.

! Three hundred babies come out of each egg laid by a chalcid fly wasp! !

Are insects of any use to us?

Some insects are very useful to us. Bees make honey. Silkworms make silk, which we use for clothing. An insect called the lac gives off a sticky liquid that we use to make shellac. Bees, butterflies, moths, and other insects carry the yellow dust called pollen from flower to flower. Then the plants can grow seeds, which will become new plants. We eat some of these seeds in fruits and vegetables, and we plant some seeds for new crops.

There are also many harmful insects that spread disease, damage plants, and eat clothing and furniture. And there are insects, such as the mosquito, that bite us. But other insects help to get rid of these harmful ones. For example, the praying mantis and the ladybug eat large numbers of harmful insects.

Why are insects so thin?

Insects are very thin because of the way they breathe. They have no lungs for breathing air. Instead, they breathe air through tiny holes in their bodies. The air cannot travel very far through these holes. If an insect were fat, air could not reach every part of its body. The insect could not live. So, in order to get air into all parts of their bodies, insects must be very skinny.

What was the largest insect ever to live?

Many millions of years ago there lived a giant dragonfly whose body was 15 inches long. Its wings measured more than 27 inches from the tip of one wing to the tip of another. However, this insect's body was only about a quarter of an inch thick. If the dragonfly had been fatter, it would not have been able to breathe.

IT'S A BIRD!
IT'S THE RED BARON!!
IT'S A DRAGONFLY!!!

What is the largest insect living today?

The largest insect is a type of "walking stick" that lives in the tropics. It is very long and skinny, and it looks a lot like a twig when it rests on a tree. This walking stick sometimes grows to be nearly 13 inches long.

Where do insects go in winter?

Most insects die at the end of the summer. But they leave many eggs to hatch in the spring. Bumblebees die, but they don't leave eggs. Instead, their queen stays alive all winter. She sleeps underground until spring. Then she comes out and starts laying eggs. Other insects also stay alive during the winter. These sleep underground or in a barn or cellar for the winter months. Crickets and mosquitoes do this. Ants do, too. But ants come out on warm, sunny winter days. Monarch butterflies are like birds. They fly south to warmer places for the winter.

Some monarch butterflies travel more than 2,000 miles to the south for the winter!

What insects act the most like people?

Ants act the most like people. They live in nests that are much like cities. Often the nests are built underground and are full of tunnels. They may have roads leading to and from the entrance. Inside the city, ants keep busy doing different jobs. Some clean the tunnels, some take care of babies, and some guard the city. Others go outside and gather food.

There are ants that fight wars. There are ants that have slaves. There are even ants that keep other insects as pets. Some kinds of ants grow their own food in gardens. Others keep "ant cows."

What is an "ant cow"?

An ant cow is another name for an insect called an aphid (AY-fid). Aphids make a sweet liquid called honeydew. Certain kinds of ants keep aphids and "milk" them, just as farmers keep cows. An ant farmer uses its feelers to stroke an aphid's sides. The aphid then lets out a drop of honeydew for the ant to drink.

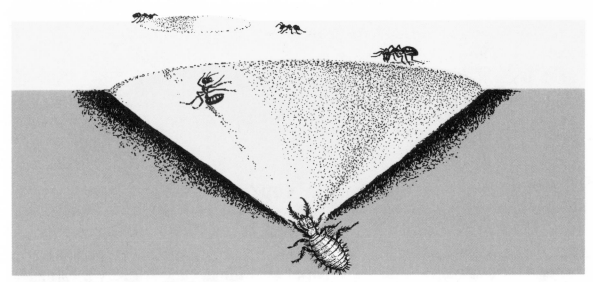

What is a doodlebug?

A doodlebug is another name for a young antlion. An antlion is not an ant and it's not a lion. It is an insect that—to an ant—might seem as ferocious as a lion seems to us.

In the early part of its life, an antlion digs a pit in sand and buries itself at the bottom. Only its head sticks out. It waits for an ant to fall into the pit. When one does, the antlion kills it and sucks the juices out of its body.

Are ladybugs useful?

Yes, ladybugs are very useful because they eat aphids. Although ants like aphids, people don't. Aphids drink the juices in plants and ruin farmers' crops. Ladybugs eat so many aphids that people use them to control the pests. Some farmers raise ladybugs and let them go in places where aphids are eating the crops.

How can a fly walk on the ceiling?

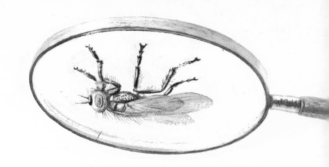

A fly can walk upside down on the ceiling because of the pads on each of its six feet. If you look at a fly with a magnifying glass, you can see these pads clearly. Some scientists think that the fly stays on the ceiling because the pads are sticky. Others believe that the curved pads flatten out against the ceiling and hold on the way suction cups do.

Will "darning needles" harm you?

"Darning needles" look like dangerous insects. But they are really perfectly harmless. In fact, they are very helpful to us. They eat many insect pests, such as flies and mosquitoes. A darning needle's real name is dragonfly.

A dragonfly can keep up with a car moving at 50 miles an hour!

How do fireflies light up?

Fireflies make two special juices in their bodies. When these juices mix together with air, fireflies light up. Scientists are not sure why fireflies make this light. But they think that it is probably a signal to attract a mate.

How do bees make honey?

Only one kind of bee—the honeybee—makes honey. First a honeybee goes to flowers to get nectar. Nectar is a sweet liquid found inside the flowers. A bee drinks the nectar and stores it in its "honey stomach." The honey stomach is not the same stomach that the bee uses to digest its food. It is a special stomach where the nectar is changed into watery honey.

The bee then flies back to its hive. It sucks up the watery honey from its honey stomach, and places the honey in little cubbyholes called cells. In the cells, the water dries out of the honey. At last the honey is finished.

One thousand bees must work their entire lives to make one pound of honey!

Why do bees buzz?

The sound of a bee buzzing is nothing more than the sound of its wings moving. So when a bee flies, you hear the buzzzzz.

Why do bees sting?

Answer: Bees sting because they are mean. That is why bees sting.

Sally is wrong. Bees are not mean. Bees sting in order to protect themselves from enemies. If you don't bother a bee, it will usually not feel threatened by you, and it will not sting you. However, the smell of certain perfumes may cause a bee to sting. So if you are wearing perfume, watch out!

Does a bee die when it stings you?

Only honeybees die when they sting you. No other bees do. Most of the bees that sting have smooth stingers. After one of them stings you, its stinger slips right out of your flesh. But the honeybee's stinger has a hook at the end of it. When the honeybee flies away after stinging you, the stinger stays hooked into your flesh. Soft parts of the bee's body pull off with the stinger. The honeybee soon dies.

How dangerous is the sting of a bee or a wasp?

The sting of a bee or wasp is usually not dangerous to people. Most of the time the sting hurts a lot, and the area around the sting swells up. But after a while the pain goes away, and so does the swelling. Some people, however, are allergic to the sting. They may break out in a rash, or their eyes and lips may swell up. A few people are so allergic to stings that they have trouble breathing and must quickly see a doctor. This extra strong reaction is not very common.

IGNORE THEM, LINUS. THEY DON'T EVEN LIKE PEANUT BUTTER.

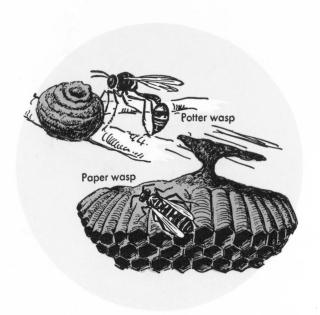

Potter wasp

Paper wasp

What are hornets and yellowjackets?

Hornets and yellowjackets are two of the most familiar kinds of wasps. As wasps, they are related to bees, and are known for their love of fruit juices and their painful stings. Some kinds of wasps live all alone. Others, including hornets and yellowjackets, live in groups as honeybees do. Like all wasps, hornets and yellowjackets are helpful insects. The adults feed their babies insects that are harmful to people and crops.

What is a wasp's nest made of?

Different kinds of wasps make different kinds of nests. Paper wasps, including hornets and yellowjackets, build their nests of paper. They make the paper by chewing up wood. Some wasps make their nests from mud. Mud daubers build rows of mud cells in protected places, such as under bridges and roofs of buildings. Potter wasps attach their mud nests to plants. Theirs look just like tiny clay pots! Carpenter wasps dig tunnels in wood for their nests. Digger wasps dig tunnels in the ground.

Why do mosquito bites itch?

If your mosquito bites itch, you must be allergic to the liquid the mosquito puts under your skin. Only female mosquitoes bite. When one bites you, she pricks your skin with a long, thin part of her mouth. Then she sucks some of your blood for food. The mosquito has a special liquid in her mouth to keep your blood thin and easy to suck. Some of this liquid gets under your skin. It causes the bite to swell and itch—but only if you are allergic to the liquid. Some lucky people are not allergic and never itch at all from mosquito bites!

How did the praying mantis get its name?

When a praying mantis holds its front legs up together, it looks as if it is praying. However, this insect is not praying at all. It is waiting for a smaller insect to come by, so that it can grab the insect with its front legs. The praying mantis will crush the insect and eat it. People like the praying mantis because it eats many insects that harm our crops and carry diseases.

GOOD GRIEF, I WISH MY PRAYING MANTIS WOULD CATCH THAT NOISY MOSQUITO.

Some people tie praying mantises to their beds to catch pesty insects!

73

What is the difference between a moth and a butterfly?

Moths usually fly at night and butterflies fly during the day. The body of a moth is thick and hairy. The body of a butterfly is thin and not at all hairy. The feelers of a butterfly are slender and have little knobs at the ends. The moth's feelers don't have these knobs, and they are often quite feathery. Both moths and butterflies can be beautifully colored, but butterflies' colors are brighter.

How does a caterpillar turn into a butterfly?

When a butterfly egg hatches, out comes a wormlike creature called a caterpillar. The caterpillar eats a lot of food and grows big. Then it attaches itself to a twig and grows a hard skin. Now it is called a chrysalis (KRIS-uh-lis). For weeks, or sometimes months, the chrysalis stays very still. But inside the hard covering, many changes are slowly taking place. Four wings, six legs, feelers, and new and different eyes are forming. Spring comes, and the covering splits open. A butterfly with tiny damp wings comes out. It hangs on a twig until its wings dry out. Then it is ready to fly away.

  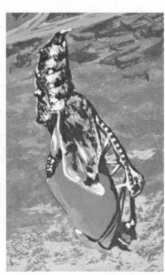 

Don't butterflies spin cocoons?

No, butterflies do not spin cocoons. But moths do. When a moth caterpillar is big enough, it spins a protective case around itself. This case is called a cocoon. The cocoon is spun of silk, which the caterpillar makes in its body. The caterpillar rests inside its cocoon and slowly changes into a moth. Then, like the butterfly, the moth comes out of its covering and soon flies away.

COCOON

Silkworm moth and eggs

Young silkworms

Silkworms spinning cocoons

Open cocoon

How do we get silk from silkworms?

The silkworm is really a caterpillar that will someday become a small pale-gray moth. It spins a cocoon of silk just as other moth caterpillars do. But its silk is especially fine.

The silkworm's silk comes out of its mouth as a thread of gluey liquid. The thread hardens as soon as it touches the air. The thread is often as long as 1,000 feet! The caterpillar winds the thread around and around its body to form a cocoon.

To get the silk, people heat the cocoon and kill the animal inside. Next they put the cocoon in warm water to soften the gum that holds the threads in place. Then they can unwind the thread. From the thread, fine silk material is woven.

WOODSTOCK WOULD HAVE MADE A LOUSY MOTH!

Why do moths gather around light bulbs at night?

Many insects are attracted to light. They have an instinct to go toward it. A moth is one of these insects. When a light goes on, a moth is drawn to it. The moth can't stay away. Since moths are awake at night, you will often see a group of them flying around and around a light bulb.

The sphinx moth curls up its long tongue and uses it as a pillow!

Why do moths eat your clothes?

Actually, moths don't eat your clothes. Certain moth caterpillars eat them. Clothes are their food. They especially like wool and fur. These caterpillars get into your closet or drawer if a female moth lays her eggs there. When the eggs hatch, the hungry little caterpillars come out and go to work on your clothes.

How do worms get into apples?

They are born there! In the middle of summer, when apples are growing on apple trees, female flies lay their eggs inside some of the apples. The eggs hatch into tiny worms called larvae (LAR-vee), which begin eating the apples. If you bite into one of these apples, you will find a worm. If no one picks the apples, they fall off the trees in the autumn. The larvae crawl out and bury themselves in the ground. A hard skin forms around each one. The next summer, a fly comes out of the skin.

How do crickets chirp?

Crickets don't use their mouths or throats to make their chirping sound. They rub their wings together. Only male crickets make this sound. They attract female crickets with it.

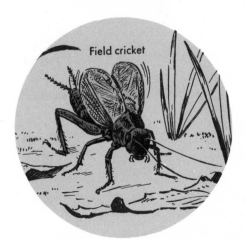

Field cricket

Why do termites eat the frames of our houses?

Termites don't eat the wooden frames of houses just because they are hungry. They are also building their homes in the wood. They chew holes that they use as rooms to live in. They line the holes with chewed-up wood that they have made into a kind of clay.

Wood-eating termites damage more than the frames of houses. They eat wooden bridges, fences, and boats. If they get inside houses, they eat furniture, books, and paper. Look what termites did to Snoopy's house!

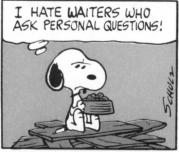

Tiny, tiny animals live inside every termite and help it digest wood!

Why can't we get rid of cockroaches?

Cockroaches are experts at staying alive. They can eat almost anything—garbage, soap, book bindings, even television wires! They have been around since the days of the dinosaurs — many millions of years. For a long time, people have been trying to kill off cockroaches because they bring germs into homes and restaurants. Although it is possible to get rid of them for a while, they usually return. Poisons kill cockroaches, but cockroach babies are often born immune to the same poison that killed their parents. This means that the babies cannot be killed by that poison.

Cockroaches like damp and dirty places best. So a clean, dry house may discourage them from coming in. However, they will probably be around somewhere for the next few million years.

Spider

Are spiders insects?

No, spiders are not insects, although they are close relatives. Insects have six legs. Spiders have eight. An insect's body has three main parts. A spider's body has only two. Most insects have feelers and wings. Spiders don't have either. Spiders belong to the group of animals called arachnids (uh-RACK-nids).

Insect

How does a spider spin a web?

A spider spins a web out of silk that it makes inside its body. The silk comes out in very thin liquid threads. As soon as a thread touches air, it hardens. Some of the threads are sticky and some are not. The spider attaches the threads to a tree or house in a particular pattern. One kind of web you may have seen is called an orb web. It looks something like a wheel. Flies and other insects get caught in the sticky threads of the "wheel." The spider then kills the insects and eats them.

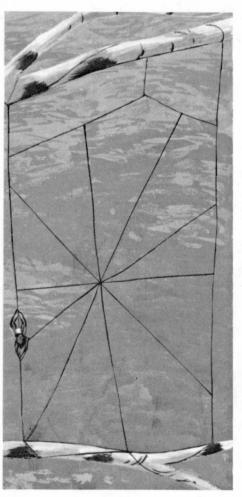

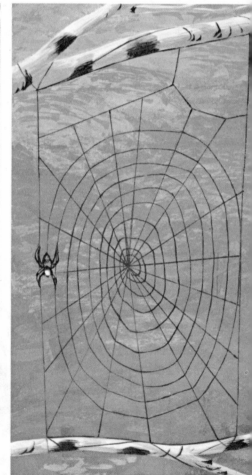

Why aren't spiders caught in their own webs?

A spider is careful to walk only on the non-sticky threads of its web. But even if it does slip and touch the sticky threads, it isn't caught. It is protected by an oily covering on its body.

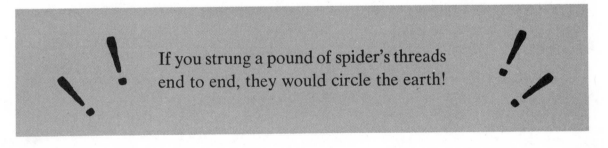

If you strung a pound of spider's threads end to end, they would circle the earth!

What is a daddy-longlegs?

A daddy-longlegs is a relative of the spider, but it does not spin a web. You can easily recognize a daddy-longlegs by its tiny body and eight very long, skinny legs. If it loses one of these legs, it will grow a new one!

Fish

How many kinds of fish are there?

Scientists have found about 21,000 different kinds of fish. All of them are alike in some ways. They all have bones inside their bodies, and they all live in water. They are all cold-blooded, which means that their body temperature is the same as the water temperature. Almost all fish have fins, which help them swim. And most have scales to protect their bodies.

Yet different kinds of fish look amazingly different. Fish are every color you can imagine—red, green, gray, yellow, purple, orange, blue, and brown. Some have stripes, some have spots, and others have fancy patterns. Many fish are very tiny and many others are very large. Fish vary in shape from short and fat to long and skinny. Some even look like snakes.

How can fish breathe in water?

Fish can breathe in water because of the way their bodies are made. Like all animals, fish need to breathe the gas called oxygen in order to live. Oxygen is in the air and in the water, too. Land animals have lungs, which can take oxygen from air but not from water. Fish don't have lungs. They have gills. Gills can take oxygen from water.

When a fish breathes, it takes water in through its mouth. The water then flows through the gills, which take oxygen out of it. Then the water goes out of the fish's body through little openings on each side of its head.

Water with oxygen in it.

Can any fish live out of water?

Yes, a few fish can live out of water—some for hours, some for days, and some for years! Mudskippers hop around on land and even climb trees. So do climbing perch. Walking catfish can crawl along the ground and breathe air for a few days at a time.

The most amazing fish, though, is the lungfish. In summer, the streams where it lives often dry up. So the lungfish curls up in a ball of mud at the bottom of a stream. It goes to sleep for months or maybe even for years—until the rains come again. While it is sleeping, the lungfish breathes air through a little hole it has made in the mudball. In spite of its name, the lungfish does not have lungs. It has gills, and a special air bladder that it uses to breathe air.

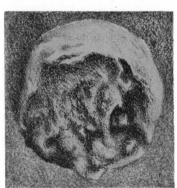

Lungfish in a mudball

Lungfish

83

SHHHH YOU'LL WAKE UP THE FISH

How can fish live in a frozen pond?

If the pond is frozen solid from top to bottom, then fish can *not* live there. Solid ice will not give fish the oxygen they need to keep alive. But usually when we talk about a frozen pond, we mean one with just a covering of ice. This sheet of ice has water below it, and so fish can live in the pond. They usually stay near the bottom of the pond, where the temperature is warmer than near the top.

Do fish sleep?

Most fish do sleep—but with their eyes open! Fish cannot close their eyes, because they have no eyelids. When sleeping, many fish lie on their side or belly at the bottom of the pond, river, or aquarium where they live. The fish that don't sleep take rests. They just stop swimming and stay in one place for a while.

 A grown-up flounder has both eyes on one side of its head!

What do fish eat?

Because so many other water creatures are looking for food, too, most fish eat just about anything they can get. They eat insects, worms, and water animals, including other fish. Some even eat their own babies. There are fish that eat plants, too. But not many eat just plants.

84

Does a fish feel pain when caught on a hook?

A hooked fish feels very little pain. In order for any animal to feel pain, it must have many nerves in the area that is hurt. The nerves send a message of pain to the animal's brain. A fish has very few nerves around its mouth, where it usually gets hooked. So it cannot feel very much there.

Do fish have voices?

A few do. A fish called the croaker makes a deep, grumpy-sounding "gur-rumph." The sound is made in the fish's belly and is a lot like the noise a bullfrog makes. A fish called the grunting catfish makes a sound, too—but only when you take it out of the water.

School of Fish

What is a school of fish?

A school of fish is not a place where fish learn things. Fish schools are simply groups of fish that stay together. In a school, fish have more protection against hungry enemies. Each school is made up of one kind of fish. You will never find bluefish and herring together in one school. You will never even find baby fish in the same school as adult fish.

How many fish are in a school?

The number of fish in one school can vary from about 25 in a school of tuna to hundreds of millions in a school of sardines.

How fast can fish swim?

The fastest fish is the sailfish, which sometimes swims at more than 60 miles an hour. A few fish can swim between 30 and 45 miles an hour. Most are much slower. A small trout moves along at only 4 miles an hour. But it still swims faster than you do!

THE SAILFISH IS THE FASTEST FISH!

Do all fish swim?

One kind of fish does not swim. It walks along the sand at the bottom of the water. This is the batfish. The batfish lives in shallow salt water. Its fins are not really fins—they are more like legs. The batfish uses them to walk around.

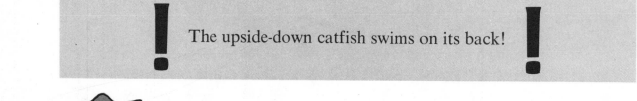

! The upside-down catfish swims on its back! !

STOCKED WITH PYGMY GOBY

What fish is the smallest?

The pygmy goby is the smallest adult fish. It hardly ever grows longer than one-third of an inch, which is only this long: ——— .

What fish is the biggest?

The whale shark is the biggest fish. It can grow up to 59 feet long. And it can weigh up to 15 tons—more than twice as much as an African elephant!

Are sharks dangerous?

Yes, many of them are dangerous. These sharks will eat anything that comes their way, including people. Even a shark's skin is dangerous. It is covered with tiny sharp spines that are like little teeth. You can get hurt just brushing against a shark.

Surprisingly, the biggest shark, the whale shark, is not dangerous to people. It eats only small plants and small water animals.

How did the shark get its name?

The word "shark" comes to us from a Latin word meaning sharp teeth!

Is any fish more dangerous than a shark?

A piranha (pih-RAHN-yuh) may be more dangerous than a shark. Although piranhas are small, they have very sharp teeth. These fish travel in schools of thousands and attack all at once. A school of piranhas can eat all the flesh of a big fish, or even a human, in just a few minutes. Piranhas live only in the Amazon region of South America.

Do flying fish really fly?

No, flying fish do not really fly. They glide through the air. Flying would mean that they flapped their fins the way a bird flaps its wings. But these fish don't move their fins when they are out of the water. They simply spread wide their large fins and sail through the air at great speed. Flying fish glide above the water in order to escape from their enemies, which are mostly dolphins.

When a flying fish wants to glide, it swims very quickly to the top of the water. As its head comes out of the water, the fish gives a powerful flip of its tail. This pushes it into the air. The fish can glide above the sea for two or three hundred yards at a time.

How long can goldfish live?

At least one goldfish is known to have lived 40 years. Most goldfish can live about 17 years. Pet goldfish in aquariums don't usually live so long. They often die young from dirty water or a sudden change in water temperature.

In a large pond, a goldfish can grow to be as long as your arm!

What do baby eels look like?

Baby eels don't look at all like their parents. They look like tiny glass leaves. But as they grow, they change into the long, thin fish we recognize as eels.

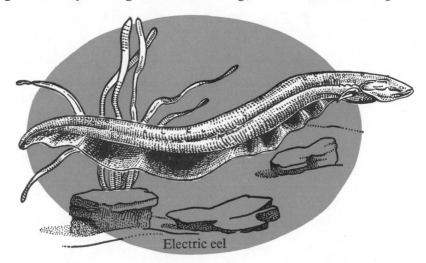

Electric eel

What does an electric eel do with its electricity?

An electric eel uses the electricity in its body to catch food and to scare off enemies. This fish's body is something like a car battery. It makes and stores electricity, which the eel can turn on and off. The shock the eel gives can be strong enough to throw a man across a room. Small water animals are stunned by the shock and can't get away from the hungry eel. Scientists are still trying to find out exactly how this fish makes its electricity.

89

Is a sea horse a fish?

Yes, a sea horse is a fish, even though it doesn't look much like one. Except for its head, it doesn't look much like a horse either. A sea horse doesn't move the way most fish do. It swims in an upright position, with its head up and its tail pointing down. The one fin on its back moves very quickly and pushes the sea horse along in the water.

Baby sea horses hatch inside a pocket on their **father's** belly!

Are there any sea serpents?

Yes, there are sea serpents, but they are not monsters. They are simply snakes that live in the sea or fish that have snakelike bodies. One of these fish is the oarfish. It grows to be 25 or 30 feet long and has bright red spines sticking out of its head. It looks pretty frightening but is really quite harmless.

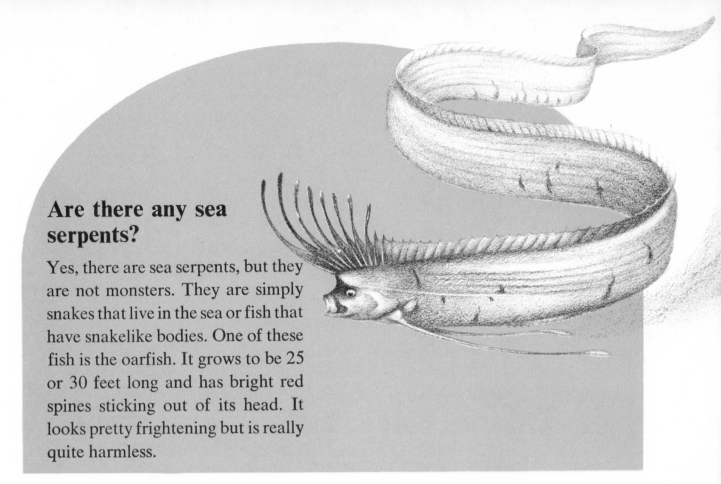

What is a mermaid?

The word "mermaid" means sea maiden. Mermaids are supposed to be beautiful sea creatures who are half human and half fish. But mermaids exist only in folk tales. They are not real.

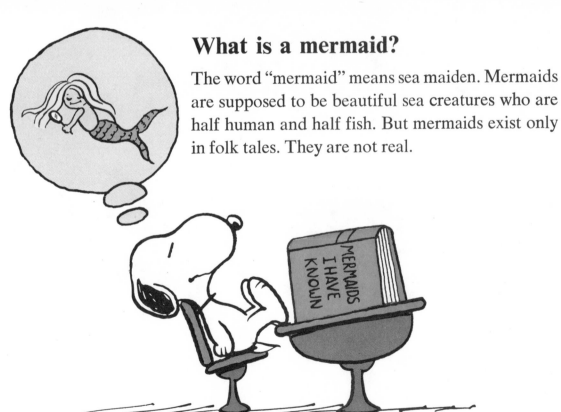

Amphibians

What are amphibians?

Amphibians are animals that live double lives. Most live in the water when they are young. After they have grown up they live on land, although they return to the water to mate and lay eggs. Amphibians are born with gills for breathing in water, just like fish. Later, most of them develop lungs for breathing air. Like fish, amphibians are cold-blooded. Their bodies have the same temperature as the air or water around them.

The amphibians include frogs, toads, salamanders, and caecilians (see-SIL-ee-unz). Caecilians are blind wormlike animals that live underground when grown.

Salamander

Toad

Frog

What is a tadpole?

A tadpole is a baby frog or a baby toad. But it looks more like a fish. Tadpoles have no legs, and they have long tails. They breathe through gills the way fish do. Tadpoles are sometimes called polliwogs.

Where does the tadpole's tail go when the tadpole becomes a frog?

As a tadpole changes into a frog, its tail seems to get smaller and smaller. But the tail is not really shrinking. It is changing. It is slowly becoming part of the rest of the tadpole's body. During this time of change, the tadpole grows hind legs, and then a pair of front legs. Its gills change into lungs so it can breathe air. Toad tadpoles change in much the same way as frog tadpoles.

What's the difference between a toad and a frog?

A toad is usually a chubby creature with rough, bumpy skin and no teeth. A frog is thinner, has smooth skin, and usually has teeth. Like all amphibians, frogs and toads are born in the water and return there to mate. But many frogs also spend a large part of their adult lives in the water, while most toads do not. A frog's eggs are often found in big clumps in the water. A toad's eggs are often found in long strings, like beads.

Tree toad

Leopard frog

Can you get warts from a toad?

No, you cannot get warts by touching a toad. That is just superstition. The rough skin of a toad looks as if it is covered with warts, and that is probably why the story got started.

However, the toad is not completely harmless. When a toad is attacked by another animal, it sends out a liquid poison from the bumps on its skin. The poison hurts the attacker's mouth and may keep it from eating the toad, If you catch a toad, and it lets out some of this liquid, be careful not to rub your eyes. The liquid will make them sore. But it will not give you warts.

A toad eats about 100 insects every day!

What do frogs eat?

Luckily for us, frogs eat mosquitoes. They also eat flies, moths, beetles, small crayfish, and worms. A frog's mouth is very large. It has two rows of teeth on the upper jaw and none on the lower jaw. A frog has a long sticky tongue attached to the front, not the back, of its mouth. This tongue can be flipped out as quick as a wink to catch insects.

Do people really eat frogs' legs?

Yes, many people enjoy eating frogs' legs. The large hind legs—the jumping legs—are the ones used. They are usually cooked in butter. Most French restaurants have frogs' legs on the menu. Frogs are even raised on frog farms to supply the demand for this unusual dish.

How far can a frog jump?

The longest frog jump on record is 17 feet and 4 inches.

What is the world's largest frog?

The largest frog is the Goliath frog of West Africa. The biggest one ever caught weighed more than seven pounds and was over 32 inches long with its legs spread out.

 The world's smallest frog could fit inside a thimble!

What is the biggest amphibian?

The biggest amphibian is the giant salamander of China and Japan. One found in 1920 was five feet long and weighed almost 100 pounds!

Where do salamanders live?

Adult salamanders are never far from water. They die if they can't keep their skin moist. Some grown salamanders live in ponds and streams. Others live on land, in damp places that are cool and dark. You can find them in shady woods. Often they lie under stones or in hollow logs.

What are mud puppies, newts, and efts?

Mud puppies and newts are simply kinds of salamanders. During the time newts are living on land, they are called efts. As efts, they are orange-colored. When they go back to water to mate, they turn green.

Did You Know That...

Sometimes different kinds of animals depend on each other for survival. Inside the termite live thousands of tiny one-celled animals called protozoa (pro-tuh-ZOE-uh). The termite eats wood, the protozoa digest the wood, and the termite is then able to digest what they leave behind. The protozoa and termite are a team. They need each other. In fact, they couldn't survive without each other. This kind of relationship is called symbiosis (sim-by-OH-sis).

Puffer fish look quite ordinary when they are swimming along. But, when they are threatened by an enemy, they can expand themselves with water to several times their normal size. Then the puffer fish look much bigger and the enemy is frightened away.

Puffer fish

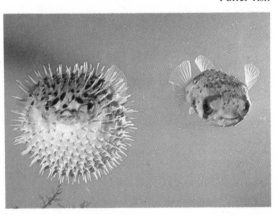

Most animals have to spend a lot of time finding food and shelter. But parasites depend on other animals. Some dogs are experts on one of the best-known parasites—the flea!

When honeybees dance in the air, it's not just for fun. They are really letting other bees from their hive know where to find food. Fellow workers watch the honeybee dance and are able to get directions that will lead them to the exact location of pollen and nectar.

The hermit crab is born without a hard shell. Because it doesn't have a home to call its own, it has to find a shell from another animal that will fit. The shell protects the crab from its enemies until it outgrows the shell. Then the crab has to find a new home that it will take wherever it scurries.

Barnacles are a kind of shellfish that spend their entire adult lives fastened to one spot. Some attach themselves to rocks. Others cling to crabs, sharks, and whales. One ship can be the home for more than 100 tons of barnacles. Sometimes barnacles have to be scraped off ship bottoms because they slow the ship's speed too much.

Camouflage (blending in with your surroundings), can be very important in the animal world. The inchworm is a real camouflage artist. When a spider comes near, the inchworm freezes and pretends to be a twig. It blends in so well that the spider will often walk right across the "twig" without suspecting a thing.

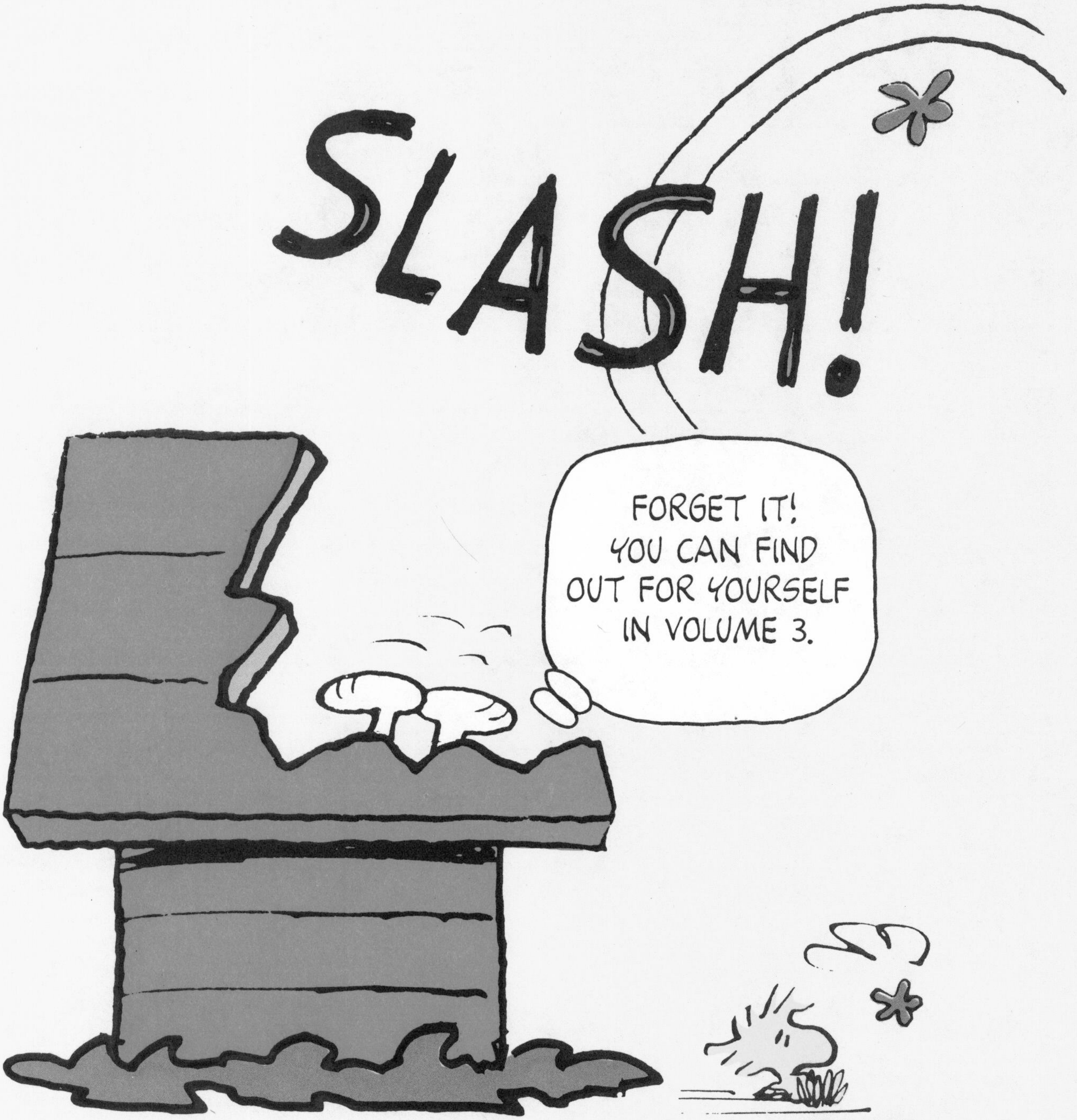
SLASH!
FORGET IT! YOU CAN FIND OUT FOR YOURSELF IN VOLUME 3.